I0388449

THE LITTLE WHITE LIE

How the Excuse of Not Feeling Like It Can
Distract You from Living the Life You Crave

CASSANDRA D. FREEMAN

PUBLISHING

Published by
WSA Publishing
301 E 57th Street, 4th fl
New York, NY 10022

Copyright © 2018 by Cassandra Freeman

All rights reserved. No part of this book may be reproduced or transmitted in any form or by in any means, electronic or mechanical, including photocopying, recording, or by any information storage and retrieval system, without the written permission of the Publisher, except where permitted by law.

Manufactured in the United States of America, or in the United Kingdom when distributed elsewhere.

Freeman, Cassandra
    The Little White Lie: How the Excuse of
    Not Feeling Like It Can Distract You from
    Living the Life You Crave
ISBN: 978-1-948181-18-1

Cover design: Joe Potter
Copyedit: Annie Preston
Interior design: Claudia Volkman
Photo credits: Kimberly Hise

www.thoughtfulinspirations.com

DEDICATION

Dedicated to every woman who has big dreams and is afraid or too comfortable to take the next step forward. Remember, your next step can be a step toward your best life. You can make it, create it, own it, and live it. Your best life starts now.

CONTENTS

Introduction 1

Part 1: Comfort Is a Lie

Chapter 1: I Don't Feel Like It.................................7

Have you ever had the thought, "I don't feel like it?" Find out how to overcome that phrase here.

Chapter 2: Avoidance..15

Get to the heart of why you have become close with comfort.

Chapter 3: Entertaining Comfort.......................23

Be careful of the company you keep. Are you spending too much time with your comfort?

Part 2: Embracing Discomfort

Chapter 4: The Hesitation Checklist................29

This one thing can keep you bonded with comfort forever.

Chapter 5: The Transformative Power of Discomfort...37

When you get a hold of this, your life will change forever.

Chapter 6: Things That Challenge Comfort...43

*Are you ready to confront your past
and gain control of your future?*

Part 3: Own It—Take Back Your Life

Chapter 7: Keys to Disabling Comfort............51

*How do you get out of your comfort zone?
Try these keys!*

Chapter 8: Recipes for Thriving in Your Dream Life..69

*Own your dream life with these quick
dream-building recipes.*

Resources..75

INTRODUCTION

As a stay-at-home mom for over ten years, I have had the pleasure of being with my boys and raising them to be great men. But I've also experienced the uneasy relationship that comes with being too comfortable. Was I just sitting around doing nothing? No. For years, with four boys under the age of five, we didn't always have the money to go places, let alone a car to get there. My husband worked crazy hours. Many days I didn't have a car, so I would walk all the way to the store to make sure I had dinner for the kids. I learned that you have to accept things as they are so you can keep your joy; you

THE LITTLE WHITE LIE

slowly wait for that next raise or for things to get just a little bit better.

Fast-forward a few years: I've started my own business. You see, I've always been a hard worker. I started speaking and making money from my products. But something weird happened. I realized that I was starting to gain weight, my relationships were drifting, I was traveling to events but never got to enjoy any of the places I was going, and I lost my determination to act. I was anxious to get out and do things that I knew I would love, because I was being tricked by that little white lie that I was telling myself: *It isn't possible... I can't do it.*

To be completely honest with you, I think that at the root of our comfort zones is the thought that we don't know if we can do this. But many times we just tell ourselves that we don't feel like it to avoid the painful reality of not believing in ourselves.

INTRODUCTION

So how did I overcome all of that? I had to go through the very same process that I'll describe in this book for you. That's right—I've already gone through this, so I know where you are and how you feel. Later in the book I'll share the actual exercises I used to create my dream life and start living it.

People come up to me all the time and say, "You look great—how did you do it? How did you get your finances together? How do you live your best life and create such happiness?" I tell them it's not a matter of not being able to do it or not wanting to do it. It's that they are too comfortable. They've become besties with being comfortable, and they live in the land of *I don't feel like it*. They've allowed their feelings to dominate their lives and strip away their dreams.

But not you. Not any longer. You are reading this because you want to move outside of your comfort zone into your best life. And it's there. It's waiting for you. It's waiting for you to take action. It's time for you to confront your comfort zone and break its limits. Rip off the warning banners, break free from any indecisiveness about moving forward, and choose freedom.

Your best life starts now.

PART I

COMFORT IS A LIE

CHAPTER 1

I DON'T FEEL LIKE IT

Did you ever wake up one morning knowing you were supposed to do something and instantly thought, *I don't feel like it*? Or maybe it's after work and you feel tired; you have so much to do. You think about cooking a healthy dinner and instead you think, *I really don't feel like cooking tonight*. So you get in your car and head to the nearest fast-food restaurant to grab something quick. Or maybe you went to bed late because you were trying to get the kids to bed, pack their lunches for tomorrow, and do something with the laundry, and then when it comes to getting up early in the morning to exercise, you hit snooze and say, "I'm too tired—I don't feel like it."

In all those moments you have a choice. Will you choose convenience or dream building?

You can either fight your feelings and take the proper actions that will lead you toward the best life for yourself or you can allow your feelings to lead you to a place of comfort, where you make decisions based on convenience instead of the big vision that you have for your life.

The phrase "I don't feel like it" reminds me of a story I heard a few years ago.

> Indecisiveness is like being in a burning building. Imagine a person standing on the top floor on the ledge. They have the fire behind

them consuming everything around it. Then they have the height of their drop. Down in front of them there's the fire truck and the fire balloon cushion they are supposed to jump into. Being indecisive is looking at the fire and saying, "I don't want to go back because I'm afraid of the fire. But I don't want to jump because I'm afraid to jump." You end up staying there, in that spot, stuck in between two choices, "Do I jump or do I go back?" (Bishop T.D. Jakes)

Telling yourself "I don't feel like it" is a lot like being stuck between two choices. One choice has the painful potential to kill your dreams and the other, more uncomfortable choice has the potential to save you so you can move on to live your best life.

THE LITTLE WHITE LIE

Many times you don't move forward in the midst of not feeling like it. You get stuck in that cycle of indecisiveness, staying frozen between two choices. Mostly it's because you want to avoid the pain of your own discomfort. But the pain of your discomfort is only an illusion—an illusion caused by your desire for comfort that keeps you in the life of mediocrity.

It's time to pull off the vale of comfort that distorts the view of your future. Releasing this distortion will renew your clarity and reveal the next steps you need to take to carry out the vision you have for your life.

But before I proceed, let's take a moment to define comfort.

Comfort is the illusion that the moment that's coming isn't going to satisfy you as much as your current situation.

I DON'T FEEL LIKE IT

Let's think about that for a moment. Comfort is an illusion because it tells you mentally that the thing you need to do is not going to satisfy you instantly. It tells you that you have plenty of time to make up for this missed time because your future aspirations take time anyway, and you have plenty of time to make it up to yourself, to your future. Well, comfort is correct to a certain extent. What you need to do won't always satisfy you instantly, especially when you filter your decisions through the eyes of your comfort instead of your future.

The illusion that comfort distributes is dangerous. Here are the things being too comfortable can cause:

Comfort causes deprivation. Your comfort deprives you of the activities and experiences you need most.

Comfort prevents growth. If you don't go

through your discomfort, you take away the possibility and opportunity to grow through it. You cannot grow to competency while you are comfortable. Growth does not occur while you're comfortable. You are not learning with purpose while you are comfortable. You are not gaining relevant, new information. Comfort drains your competency. You remain in a state of misunderstanding when you are too comfortable.

Comfort leads to a lack of self-care. You do not take care of yourself properly. When you are comfortable you often neglect your own self-care—and sometimes the care of others you are responsible for.

Comfort makes you complacent toward your aspirations. While you are comfortable you start to accept the mundane. That becomes your place of satisfaction and guilt.

Comfort causes confusion. You become

confused about what you should do next. Confusion causes you to do nothing, so you end up staying in your comfort instead of taking action.

Comfort costs you character development. Comfort corrupts your character because when you get into the mood where you don't feel like it, you stop keeping your word; you stop RSVPing; you stop doing the things you are supposed to do.

Comfort changes your conversation. Your conversation declines in quality when you are comfortable. Have you ever noticed how people who are comfortable only talk about other people, both in real life and on TV?

But comfort isn't the bad guy here. Comfort can be beneficial to people who are in pain, who have been hurt, and others who just need rest. But just like everything in life, it must be done in moderation. I think in many cases comfort is as addicting as sugar is. It's the abuse of comfort that creates the illusion. But when used right, comfort can create peace and satisfaction.

Every day you risk your future over the idea that you still have plenty of time to make your dreams happen—that your dreams will always be there, and one day you will feel like it. I'm here to send a hard reminder that you can't get that time back. People dismiss time too easily without understanding the gravity of their decision. Your time is valuable. Invest it in your present and in your future. I know you see yourself doing great things. You can do it! Invest your time. Get out of your comfort zone and start making great things happen in your life.

CHAPTER 2

AVOIDANCE

In psychology, *avoidance* is a method of withdrawal by which a person runs away from their discomfort or problems.

Sometimes comfort is the distance you place in between yourself and your dream life in order to protect yourself from the pain of progress. All growth comes with some form of discomfort. The problem is that you want the dream life, but you don't want the discomfort that comes with it.

It was John Maxwell who said, "People often have uphill hopes but downhill habits."

THE LITTLE WHITE LIE

Many times your bad habits will feed comfort. What you feed will grow and get stronger. That's why it's so easy to give in to the feeling of not feeling like it and so hard to resist it.

Avoidance is also directly related to procrastination. You procrastinate in order to bypass the pain or discomfort you might experience. Avoidance and procrastination both distract you from the responsibilities of doing the things you are supposed to do. The more you avoid those action items, the more you create a stronger desire to remain in a state of not feeling like it.

What do you find yourself doing instead of going after the things you really want in life? Do you watch television? Clean your house? Waste hours on the phone talking about absolutely nothing? What is your avoidance tactic? Some people drink. Others

AVOIDANCE

ignore phone calls. When you remain in your comfort for an excessive amount of time, stop and ask yourself, "What am I avoiding?"

People avoid their dreams by complaining about their circumstances. If they can get the focus off the pain of not living their dream and feeling stuck, they can get satisfaction from complaining and getting others to join in. Misery loves company. They get satisfaction through the acceptance of their complaints and thus avoid experiencing the pain of not living their dreams.

People avoid their dreams through drugs. Drugs provide pleasure as a substitute from the pain of not living their dream.

Others avoid the pain of not living their own dream through talking others out of theirs. When they successfully talk you out of your dreams, it makes them feel better for not achieving theirs. It reaffirms and validates their need for approval about neglecting their own dreams. They do this by acting like their dreams don't exist. Like it doesn't matter. Have you ever seen someone shrug their shoulders because they have an attitude? This type of behavior allows them to avoid the reality that they really do care about their dreams. If they can convince themselves that they do not care, it eases the pain of not taking action.

The Next Level

You will often experience discomfort when you desire to elevate yourself or change something about yourself. Sometimes you can get so comfortable in your usual way of doing things that you reject anything new that goes against it. You end up protecting the very comfort you are trying to break free from.

That's why you have to constantly challenge your comfort. Take risks. Do those things that

AVOIDANCE

you know you are supposed to do even when you don't feel like doing them. Learn something new that challenges what you believe.

That's what happens when people want to purchase something that will help them become their best selves but are indecisive about the purchase. Have you ever picked up a book or some over-the-counter medicine at the store, knowing it would help you in a great way, but you weren't sure whether you should invest the money in it? Or maybe you've been trying to lose weight and you contemplate whether you should hire a personal trainer and nutritionist to get you on track? It's not just because you are nervous about spending the money. It is because it's outside of your comfort zone. You are not used to spending your money in a way that stretches you to grow. You are used to spending to protect your comfort zone so that everything feels right.

I get it. It's scary to go to the next level. I'm afraid of heights. I have no issue with riding roller coasters, but don't ask me to climb up a steep flight of stairs and look down. Oh no! It's not comfortable for me. It can be the same for you, too, as you climb your own ladder to success or to your dream life. You are used to being at a certain level of comfort. So when a decision comes to climb to higher heights, your mind says, *I'm afraid of adjusting to that new height; let's go back down where it's comfortable.*

So how do you overcome avoidance?

You overcome avoidance by being honest with yourself about what you want. Stop avoiding your dreams. They are important. The life you want to live is important.

You must also confront the very thing you are avoiding. In Chapter 7, I'll share some exercises that will help you overcome and

AVOIDANCE

gain victory over comfort so you can live life to the fullest. It is a good practice to confront comfort on a regular basis. The more you confront comfort, the more you move closer to becoming your best self and living your best life.

Take action. It's hard to challenge comfort if you aren't taking any action. I'm not sure if you are into Superman. Regardless, most people are familiar with Superman's major strengths and weaknesses. One of his major weaknesses is kryptonite—it disables him. That's the same thing action does to comfort! It disables comfort. The more you take action, the more you disable comfort and the thought of *I don't feel like it*. Action is kryptonite for your comfort.

CHAPTER 3

ENTERTAINING COMFORT

Doing anything in excess can be risky. Eating, drinking, shopping online, and even exercising, running, and hiking can have an adverse effect on your life. Too much, even of a good thing, can get in the way of you getting to where you want to be, whether it is a physical goal, an emotional goal, or something on your bucket list. Only you know where you want to be. The key to it all is self-discipline.

Now, we all want comfort and we all have different levels of what that means. No matter what it is, if you entertain your comfort excessively, you will slowly pull away from where you are going, and you gradually will lose your ability to become self-disciplined. You see, self-discipline is like a muscle. If you don't work it, it will become weak.

What I am telling you is nothing new, and I believe you know what you need to do, but like most of us you struggle to get started because it requires doing something different. It requires making a change, often involving a physical or emotional adjustment. This is a difficult task, even for the most well-meaning person.

When you get distracted with comfort, it can eliminate your necessity to be corrected. In your comfort, you dismiss any correction because it reminds you of the pain of your discomfort. In most cases, the hardest part is getting started.

ENTERTAINING COMFORT

In order to grow, comfort needs to be continually entertained. Entertainment ultimately distracts you from the discomfort you must pursue in order to achieve the life you want to live. The comfort of entertainment is a momentary distraction that dissolves any thoughts of discomfort, and so you find yourself ignoring your to-do lists. Your comfort helps you avoid the things you know you should be doing. Unfortunately, this comfort prevents growth. The point is, if you don't go through discomfort, you will never fully develop the life you desire.

Comfort deprives you of the things you need the most. The life you want to live, the life you have in your heart and mind to experience, slowly starts slipping away. But it doesn't have to be that way.

You can live your best life. You can live the life you have in your heart, the life that is waiting for you. When you decide to discipline yourself instead of entertain yourself, everything falls into place and you gain a new lease on life.

PART II

EMBRACING DISCOMFORT

CHAPTER 4

THE HESITATION CHECKLIST

Why do you hesitate when the opportunity comes to live your best life? So often it's easy to rationalize being comfortable instead of choosing to defend and work for the life you truly want to live. But it doesn't have to be that way. You can decide today that being comfortable is not going to get you to your dream. You can decide that hesitation will no longer keep you from achieving your wildest goal. From this point forward you can choose to decide to live at your best.

The truth is, everyone hesitates when

it comes to being comfortable. For some reason we just don't want to let go. It's almost like two powerful magnets that are difficult to pull apart. They can come apart, but it just takes a bit of effort. It's the same thing with our comfort. We are attracted strongly to our comfort especially if we have been constantly giving in to it. Breaking apart from this attraction is so difficult that a by-product is often hesitation.

I'm talking about that moment when you think, *I really need to go to the gym*, yet you are still sitting there thinking, *But I'd rather relax and watch television, prepare dinner, and not have to wrestle the kids in and out of the gym*. Or that moment where you think about whether you should eat what you have at home or pick up a to-go order instead. Those few moments of hesitation can change the trajectory of your journey toward your best

THE HESITATION CHECKLIST

life. You are at a crossroads. You can choose the hard choice in the moment to live your dream life—or you can choose the easy route that takes you on a long detour filled with struggle to your ultimate destination of guilt, wishes, and sorrow. Don't ignore your crossroads moment. It is a defining moment that creates an opportunity you can't get back, but it's also an opportunity to become your best self. When you waste your defining moment of hesitation with avoidance, you only end up regretting and wishing that you had pushed yourself harder. And then you continue to wonder why you can't seem to push yourself to do the things you know you want to do.

Once you realize that your moment of hesitation is a portal to your best self, you can maximize the moment and choose to step out of your comfort zone.

Use this checklist to overcome your hesitation:

D.E.C.I.D.E. Checklist
Step One:
D is drive toward it.
Take small steps toward the task.
Examples include:

- Timing yourself for five minutes to do a task and racing against the clock to see how much you can get done.
- Wearing your workout clothes to bed so you have less excuses in the morning.

Step Two:
E is evaluate honestly.
Ask yourself during your moment of hesitation, "Is this something I truly need to act on?"

THE HESITATION CHECKLIST

Step Three:
C is consider your strengths.

Martin Seligman, the founder of Positive Psychology, tells a story of how one of his students had to walk about four blocks from class back to his home. The student often complained that while he enjoyed the trip to class, he didn't like his trip home. He never looked forward to it. So Seligman suggested that his student choose one of his strengths and apply it to that moment.

I have used this principle in my own life. When it comes to accounting, numbers, and budgeting, I will often use colors and express my creativity instead of creating another sheet full of black-and-white numbers.

Choose something you either love to

do or one of your strengths and apply it to what you have to do.

Step Four:
I is ignore distractions.
If you are trying to take action and people keep interrupting you or your phone keeps ringing, hit ignore. Tell people you can't talk right now because you have somewhere to be.

Step Five:
D is drop all distractions, doubts, and hesitations.
Sometimes *you* are the distraction. You could be playing with your phone when you know you should be doing something else, or watching TV when you could be working out. You need to

drop your phone and the remote control and make a move toward your dream life. Literally drop everything and move.

Step Six:
E is express how you feel afterward.
Whether you decide to take action at your hesitation crossroads or not, you need to express how you felt afterward. This will help you to see how your decision to either take action or not truly makes you feel. Write it down and read it the next time you don't feel like it.

CHAPTER 5

THE TRANSFORMATIONAL POWER OF DISCOMFORT

Discomfort is a part of every transformation. Think of a mother having contractions before she gives birth. Or an athlete in the middle of training for their big event. Or a butterfly pushing out of a cocoon. These are all transformations that require discomfort just before a major breakthrough. And it's the same for your life as well. In order to break through to your dream life, you must be willing to get a little uncomfortable.

Discomfort has been given a bad name.

THE LITTLE WHITE LIE

It's mostly due to the possibility of pain. But not all discomfort causes pain. I'm a mother, and I know that any mother who has given birth understands pain and discomfort, but sometimes we can fail to discern between the two. Sometimes something that is uncomfortable is not painful. It just feels awkward. That's the state a person is in when they say, "I don't feel like it." You are assuming that your discomfort will cause you unnecessary pain, but really it's the complete opposite.

The pain comes when you choose not to thrive outside of your comfort zone. Have you ever experienced guilt or regret after you have remained within your comfort zone instead of acting on your dream life? That's because choosing to remain in your comfort zone causes you the real pain.

But most of the time it's not seen that

way because we cannot see past our present feelings of not feeling like it.

The discomfort you experience trying to avoid your dream life is a feeling of uneasiness or awkwardness. Once you get past the awkwardness, the miraculous happens. With every step forward you gain confidence to live and build your dream journey. The discomfort of taking action causes you to rise to the occasion. Discomfort is the mountain you climb to reach the pinnacle of your success.

You can get used to discomfort. Think about it. Everything you have done or learned has been uncomfortable at some point. But you have mastered it to the point where it has become your new comfort. Life is about growing, evolving, elevating yourself, and establishing new levels of comfort.

So, what happens when you are willing to get uncomfortable and do things that you would not normally do? What happens when you are willing to establish new comfort zones? You excel at amazing rates toward your dream life. You build and gain momentum to keep moving forward. You find a new joy within yourself.

Discomfort can be transformational. It can create the most dramatic changes within you if you allow it to. How do you allow it? You give way to it. You allow it to manifest whenever you start to take action, and the more you take action, that's when the real magic happens. The more you take action, the more you will establish new levels of comfort. With every new level of established comfort comes a new level of success.

Transformation is never easy. Yet nothing easy is ever worth it. You've got to push your way toward new comforts, new successes, and you've got to break through those barriers that attempt to keep you within your comfort zone. It's your time to transform. It's your time to break through and accomplish all you have set out to achieve.

CHAPTER 6

THINGS THAT CHALLENGE COMFORT

So many things a person does can feed comfort without even knowing it. But there are also things that can disrupt comfort and decrease the likelihood of its success. So how do you challenge comfort so you can overcome it and move closer to the life you dream of?

Action

Although not the easiest of the bunch to do, action is the most effective. The more you act outside of your comfort zone, the more you grow and the more you build the discipline and steadfastness to keep moving. It becomes so much easier to ignore being comfortable with every action you take.

Commitment

You must be truly committed to the life you want to live, to creating true change. Most people are more committed to their feelings than they are to their dream life. They are more committed to enjoying a few moments of television than to their future. In order to challenge your comfort, you must decide that no matter what, you will not sit by the wayside and watch others live their dream lives while you merely wish for yours. You are going to get in the game and choose to not sit back in your comfortable chair or bed and allow life to pass you by. Decide today to be

THINGS THAT CHALLENGE COMFORT

more committed to real change than to false comfort.

Vision

Your vision is what drives you. It keeps your actions steadfast and consistent. But you can't just write your vision and speak it only once. You have to know your vision. Once you write it down, you should speak it, read it, and visualize it daily. The more you do this, the more you will be driven to take actions in alignment with your vision.

Mentorship

Mentors push and stretch you. They hold you accountable so you begin moving toward your dream life. With the right mentor in your life, you can be stretched to move out of your comfort zone and into success.

THE LITTLE WHITE LIE

Reading and Learning Something New

You might think you have no time to read or learn. I am going to challenge you on that. I guarantee that you do. Reading and learning is one of the biggest things you can do to confront comfort. It's hard to stay comfortable with new information. New information inspires new ideas, it creates momentum to act, and it provides you with new perspectives. These are all ingredients that cause you to be passionate and move toward a new thing. And new things challenge comfort. Have you ever made a new purchase and felt comfortable? You always experience either excitement to use your purchase or you feel nervous about it. That's how you feel when you start to move outside of your comfort zone—either you are eager to experience it or hesitant. It's about introducing something new. Whenever you introduce something new to your comfortable situation, you will find yourself moving away from your comfort.

Accountability

Have you ever been down and out and had a friend cheer you up? Or had someone keep you on track with your goals? That's the power of accountability. Accountability helps you to push pass your comfort and move right into action. The people who hold you accountable keep you from basking in your comfort so you can stay focused on your dream life.

PART III

OWN IT—TAKE BACK YOUR LIFE

CHAPTER 7

KEYS TO DISABLING COMFORT

So how do you overcome comfort? How do you disable it so you can launch fully into your dream life and live the life you were created to live? The following exercises will help you do just that.

Exercise One: Values and Beliefs Stairway

Your values and beliefs are those things that are important to you and true for you. When you look at your life, ask yourself, "What do I believe my life should look like? What do I believe I should experience? If I could leave a legacy that outlasts me, what would that legacy be?"

Keeping your answers in mind, follow the instructional steps below to complete your values and beliefs stairway.

This exercise will help you to identify your values and beliefs because the more you understand what truly matters to you, the more you choose it. You will find that after you make a decision and feel regretful, it is because that decision was made outside of your value system. But when you make decisions within the values you've named, you will feel the excitement and satisfaction of your decision.

Step One: Create a list from one to eight (with one being the most important) of everything you believe your life should be outside of

KEYS TO DISABLING COMFORT

your comfort zone. What would you include if you decided that regardless of how you feel, regardless of if I don't feel like it, you're going to take action anyway and do it with ease? Name the characteristics and experiences of what your life would look like.

> *Tip 1:* It can be easier to start with a broad belief at number eight and work your way up to what matters most.
>
> *Tip 2:* You can also ask yourself: "Ultimately, what do I want to experience in life?" Then ask yourself why. Ask yourself, "What do I value?" What do I believe about myself and my life?
>
> *Tip 3:* Time yourself. Give yourself three to five minutes. Set an alarm and write out your list.

THE LITTLE WHITE LIE

For example, a sample list might look like this:

1. Living out my purpose
2. Giving back
3. Family and friends
4. Healthy living
5. I believe that it's in me to live my dream life because I am determined.
6. I believe that my life is meant to be lived and not wasted.
7. Living my dream life is a requirement for experiencing joy.
8. I always find the courage to act on my dreams.

Step Two: Place your values in the stairway. Add the most important values on step 1, all the way down to the least in step 8.

KEYS TO DISABLING COMFORT

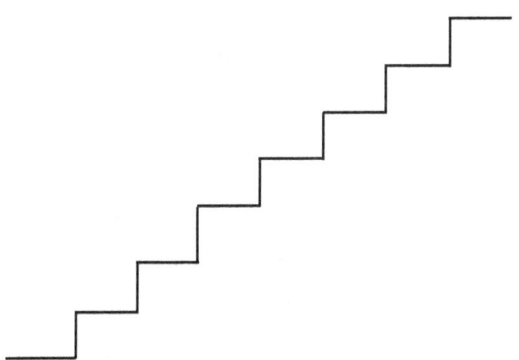

Step Three: After you have your list, refer back to it often. The more you look at it, the more it gets ingrained in you. That way, before you make a decision, you will find yourself asking, "Does this fit my value system?"

Exercise Two: Nonnegotiables

In order to get out of your comfort zone, you must set some nonnegotiables. Otherwise you will look back and see a life dedicated to things you never wanted to invest your time in. Your nonnegotiables are things that you choose to commit to that you will not sacrifice. Once you put these nonnegotiables in place, those times when you usually would feel indecisive will be a breeze. You will have decided that you are not going to sacrifice these things for anyone, not even yourself.

On the next page you will find a chart you can fill out. In the first column, list things you are not willing to sacrifice, things you are not willing to give up. In the second column, list things that do not deserve your time, things you no longer want in your life. Take a few minutes and fill this information out.

KEYS TO DISABLING COMFORT

I WILL NOT SACRIFICE	I WILL SACRIFICE
Example: Healthy Eating	Example: Family Drama

Exercise Three: Create a Not to Do List

Some days you may feel more motivated than others to take action. On the days you feel less motivated, I encourage you to create a Not to Do List. This is a list of things that you refuse to do and that you are determined will not take up your time. This list works wonders. Use it whenever you need to.

You can use a simple sheet of paper or a notepad to create your Not to Do List. You can also purchase a Not to Do List in Thoughtful Inspiration's online shop.

> **Example: Not to Do List**
> - I will not get caught up in unnecessary phone conversations.
> - I will not be on Facebook today.
> - I will not be texting people back before 3:00 p.m.

Exercise Four: Create a Dream Prosperity Plan

A Dream Prosperity Plan is the plan you have for your dream life. It is your ultimate master plan to create the life you want outside of your comfort zone. Let's begin.

KEYS TO DISABLING COMFORT

Step One: Write out what you want in life and two things you can do consistently to get it. Make these two things as clear as possible. They should be action steps that tell you exactly what you need to do and lead you where you want to go. Do this as many times as you need to until you cannot think of any other experiences you want.

For example:

- What I want: To travel more.
- What I need to do: Create a bank account for my travel funds. Choose where I want to go first.

Step Two: Write out the type of person you want to become. When you think about your future self, what and who do you see? Write the characteristics of the person below.

Here are your examples:

THE LITTLE WHITE LIE

- Who I want to become: A great mom to my four boys.
- What I need to do: Spend quality time with them that does not include me responding to business emails and calls on my phone. Teach them the lessons I've learned.

- Who I want to become: A speaker who travels around the world speaking.
- What I need to do: Practice speaking every day. Create a list of the countries and cities where I'd love to speak.

Now it's your turn. Grab your journal, notepad, or sheet of paper that you used to create your Want to Do want list and add your What Do I Want to Become list to it.

KEYS TO DISABLING COMFORT

Step Three: Write out what you want your legacy to be. How do you want to give back?

Here are your examples:

- How do I want to give back: I want to help parents go back to school with scholarships.
- What I need to do: I need to set up an account for the scholarship fund. I need to create an application for the scholarship.

- How do I want to give back: I want to help pay for tutoring for kids.
- What I need to do: Connect with schools and tutoring centers to build relationships. Collect tutoring costs sheets so I know how much it's going to cost.

THE LITTLE WHITE LIE

Step Four: Read and visualize your Dream Prosperity Plan every single day. The more you visualize your Dream Prosperity Plan, the more your life will be transformed into the very plan you have created for your life. This is no joke! You will start to see how your actions and decisions align with your Dream Prosperity Plan.

Look it over every day for thirty days. You won't even have to think about whether or not to move out of your comfort zone because you will do so automatically. You are training your brain to ignore your discomfort and indecisiveness in order to move into the abundant life that you always knew that you could have.

When I first tried my own Dream Prosperity Plan, I was skeptical. I had written that I wanted to be a marathon runner in great shape. My two action steps were that I

KEYS TO DISABLING COMFORT

would exercise every day, even if it was only walking a mile and that I would always aim to eat healthy. And guess what happened? I did it. I may not go to the gym every day, but every single day I walk one mile. Even if I am out of town speaking, I am on a treadmill or at the park somewhere walking or running. Did I have to sit there and think about whether I should exercise? Did I think, *I have a lot to do and I'm tired, so maybe tomorrow*? No. I got right up. I told myself, "I'm going to go ahead to the gym or park and walk my mile. The work will be here when I return. My health is nonnegotiable."

Exercise Five: Triggers

Surround yourself with components of your dream life. You can post photos of the places you want to travel to. You can get travel magazines. I love to see images of people doing what they love. If you want to be a great mom, clip out magazine images, or if you have them, images of you being a great mom. Get a frame for them. Get a wall quote that affirms your dream life. Many stores have great wall décor with inspirational quotes. Find a quote that talks about your dream life. This will remind you to keep working toward overcoming your comfort zone.

Tips for Disabling Comfort:
- Set a timer for five minutes when you don't feel like doing a task. Then race the clock to see how much you can get done.
- Turn up the music. Music is created to make you move. It will give you a nudge to start taking action. Before you know it, you will be dancing in

KEYS TO DISABLING COMFORT

your seat and an hour of work will be done.
- Get a coach, mentor, or accountability partner. Find someone who understands what you want to achieve and won't take no for an answer. You will need someone to push you when you don't feel like it. A tough mentor or accountability partner will keep you on track and remind you to quit slacking because you've got work to do.
- Visualize where you are going. Get an image of your outcome. Whatever your life looks outside your comfort zone, get a photo or a sketch and look at it daily. That will draw you away from not feeling like it and closer toward your dream life.

THE LITTLE WHITE LIE

You have the information and exercises you need to burst through that comfort zone! Now it's time to put it all together in a recipe of success for you.

**Dream life disclaimer: Your dream life will *not* manifest for you if you don't do the work. Effort is not only required for you to get out of your comfort zone—it is vital for your success. Do the work. Build your Dream Prosperity Plan and read it daily. You are worth it. Your dream life is worth it. You are not just reading this book to pass the time. You are reading this book because you are tired of telling yourself that cute little lie, the one we are all guilty of. That little white lie that says it's okay to do nothing, you can do it later. I'm here to tell you that it's *not* okay. You deserve better than that. It's time to respect yourself and the life you know you deserve to live. It's time for change, and that

KEYS TO DISABLING COMFORT

change starts now. So if you need to, go back and take action. And if you have already taken action, let's go create your recipe for success! Your dream life starts now!**

CHAPTER 8

RECIPE FOR THRIVING IN YOUR DREAM LIFE

This chapter combines everything you've learned from the book into an ultimate strategy to get you out of your comfort zone and into your dream life.

The key to getting out of your comfort zone and into your dream life is preparation. You have to be prepared for those moments when you won't feel like it. It's almost like being prepared for battle. You don't just go into battle. You have to be prepared with the proper uniform and weaponry. Well, this is what I would call a mental battle. You are in the mental battle of fighting with your feelings and your future. You beat a mental battle with preparation because what you train your mind to do it does. So you have to train your mind with everything we have spoken about up to now so that when you enter into that battle with your feelings, your future wins every time!

Let's talk about your recipe for success. You have to prepare, take action, and reflect.

Recipe for Success

Preparation: You prepare with the exercises from chapter 7. Create your Dream Prosperity Plan and use any one of the other exercises. Complete those. Remember, the more you do and apply, the more you manifest the life you want. Don't just race through this book and read it without taking action. Make moves.

RECIPE FOR THRIVING IN YOUR DREAM LIFE

Take action. Take responsibility for your dream life and do these exercises.

Take Action: Go about your regular activities, paying attention to when you take action and when you don't. This is important to recognize your own behavior or lack of behavior. Ask yourself when do I feel most like taking action? How did I feel when I did not take action?

Reflection: Take sixty seconds to write about how you felt about the action you took or did not take.

Bishop Rosie S. O'neal said, "Reflection is the key to wisdom." When you reflect and write down your thoughts and experiences, you grow from them in amazing ways.

Here is what your recipe for success looks like in action:

THE LITTLE WHITE LIE

Recipe for success example	
Preparation: Which exercise am I using?	Dream Prosperity Plan
Did I take action?	Yes or No
Reflection	I felt great! I walked five miles today and had a yummy, healthy snack that my nutritionist suggested!

Now it's your turn. On the next few pages you are going to create your own Recipe for Success. Every time you take action that relates to your dream life, take notes. Write down what exercises you have used and how the activities have helped you. You are a student of life now. It's time to dive in.

*Want access for more exercises and dream life strategies? Check out the resources section.

RECIPE FOR THRIVING IN YOUR DREAM LIFE

My Recipe for Success	
Preparation: Which exercise am I using?	
Did I take action?	Yes or No
Reflection	

Recipe for Success	
Preparation: Which exercise am I using?	
Did I take action?	Yes or No
Reflection	

THE LITTLE WHITE LIE

Recipe for Success	
Preparation: Which exercise am I using?	
Did I take action?	Yes or No
Reflection	

Recipe for Success	
Preparation: Which exercise am I using?	
Did I take action?	Yes or No
Reflection	

RESOURCES

The Litte White Lie Book Companion Site
You can visit thelittlewhitelie.net to get access to more great dream-building exercises.

All of the exercises included in the book, as well as additional resources, are included online.

THOUGHTFUL INSPIRATION ONLINE SHOP

Not to Do List
Stay focused on your dream life with this notepad. It will keep you from the mindset of not feeling like it, hold you accountable to your nonnegotiables, and challenge you to take fast action toward your dream life.

***The Little White Lie* Book**
Available with bulk orders. If you've loved this book, get one for a friend. Whenever I love a book that I've read, I always purchase a second copy.

Get Out of Your Comfort Zone e-course
Are you ready to step out of your comfort

zone and into your dream life? Let me show you the way in this course! Free access on the companion site at thelittlewhitelie.net.

Make It Happen e-course
This course will help you use what you've got to make your dreams happen. Sometimes when you feel like you have a lack of resources, it can cause you to remain within your comfort zone.

Aha Moment Post-it Notes
Need a place to reflect? This aha moment notepad will help you organize your thoughts and write down major thoughts that lead you toward your best life.

Daily Dream Life Checklist
Add your favorite things to your day and make every day your dream life.

JOIN THE CONVERSATION

Connect with Cassandra D. Freeman on social media @thecassandraf

on Facebook, Instagram, Pinterest, Twitter, and YouTube.

Or visit *The Little White Lie* companion site at www.thelittlewhitelie.net

BULK ORDERS

For bulk orders,
please contact Cassandra D. Freeman at
beinspired@thoughtfulinspirations.com
or call 804-464-8513.

www.ingramcontent.com/pod-product-compliance
Lightning Source LLC
Chambersburg PA
CBHW071759080526
44588CB00013B/2309